Dear Memphis

Rachel Edelman

Published in the United States of America

Library of Congress Cataloging-in-Publication Data
Edelman, Rachel, 1987–
Dear Memphis / Rachel Edelman.
ISBN-13: 979-8-9881378-2-5
Subjects: LCSH: Southern Literature; Judaism; Jewish Literature;
Women Writers; Environment—Poetry. | LCGFT: Poetry.
Library of Congress Control Number: 2023944166

Cover and interior design by Alban Fischer
Cover photograph, a door in downtown Memphis,
by author's grandfather, Dr. Thomas N. Stern

RIVER RIVER BOOKS
10 Linganore Place
Durham, NC 27707

www.RiverRiverBooks.org

Praise for DEAR MEMPHIS

"Braided within and across the primary subjects of Rachel Edelman's powerful *Dear Memphis*—diaspora, racial and social injustice, family, place—is an ongoing meditation on the complexities of memory. On the paradox of memory, which like a road map of a city one no longer lives in, holds absence and presence simultaneously. There, in the re-envisioned past, are the legends and landmarks and intersections of time. Here, through lyrics enriched by Edelman's vivid imagery and distinctive music, is timelessness. 'Beneath what I see is what I know,' she writes. *Dear Memphis* is testament to the vastness of that knowledge."

—LINDA BIERDS, author of *The Hardy Tree*

"Rachel Edelman's *Dear Memphis* is a kind of modern-day Exodus, offering haunting lyric poems that evoke experiences of dispersal and diaspora. A white Jewish woman with deep roots in Memphis, Edelman speaks searingly of 'what she knows of the South' and its racial history, one in which she is uneasily embedded. Whether arriving out of personal, biblical, historical, or political stories of migration, Edelman's poems are piercingly self-aware. This is a work of moving lamentation, undergirded by the poet's sustained interest in exposing and trying to hold opposing truths: 'the country where I am / is the country I abandoned.'"

—SHARA MCCALLUM, author of *No Ruined Stone*

"In *Dear Memphis*, Rachel Edelman probes the shifting meaning of the intersection of whiteness and Jewishness in the US South. Refusing the romance of suffering, these poems enter the terrain of ongoing struggle that is history and insist that there is nothing inherently liberatory about having been oppressed. Where white Jewish accumulation takes place alongside entrenched anti-Blackness, what might the intergenerational trauma of antisemitism mean for the possibilities of solidarity? Punctuated with epistolary poems, Edelman's searching text recalls that to address is to traverse a distance and seek a closeness, that reckoning is a profound intimacy, that to leave is also the condition of return. 'Who did I choose / when I wished myself elsewhere?' Edelman asks. Holding to the possibility of transformation in encounter, *Dear Memphis* shimmers with the difficult work of love."

—CLAIRE SCHWARTZ, author of *Civil Service*

RIVER RIVER BOOKS
Durham, North Carolina

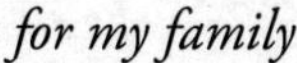

Contents

the past is a place
you cannot visit

but still—veiled—can see—

KEVIN YOUNG

Return

Descent jumps and jostles,
nausea drops me
back to the floodplain
I fled.

The taxi driver asks,
Do you have some mixed blood?

He says, *You have an old world face.*

I let my eyes flare
as he drives me
past the split
where Walnut Grove divides
cropland from greenway.

On the farm side,
heat gleams

on shoulders screened *CORRECTIONS*:
workers in the cotton
still in chains.

Past the test plots,
past the longhorn pen,
barbed wire blooms into razor—

+

Packing,
I stacked books in boxes

like green-husked walnuts
we left curbside
every spring.

On every corner, an alabaster cross:

my parents made sure
we lived among
other mezuzahs.

+

Mid-step, I stop
where sweet pea climbs the chain-link.

I sketch, invert the corners—

erase, retrace,
render the storefronts:

AVAILABLE   AVAILABLE   AVAILABLE…

follow the beams
someone felled
                    someone planed

someone nailed in place.

+

Farmers set

tomatoes bottom-up

to hide the spokes of scars
around their stems.

Sweet heirlooms
rest on a folding table, easy

like the fat gold fruit
I was born to.

I know to visit
before I point out what I want;

pass my cash, take a bag
and
Have a blessed day.

+

In her driveway Minnie hugs my neck, says
What'd you do with all your hair?

Inside, the news: a robbery, a gun bust;
she says, *They need to go get a job.*

I nod and sip my tea, the chill of her A/C blowing.
We lean almost as close

as when we'd visit over the gospel radio.
She asks what my parents won't:

When are you going to give your daddy a grandbaby?
and just like our Sundays on the phone, I say
I'm all set.

When my parents packed up, she got a pension.
My stomach growls; Minnie says
I don't need much dinner.

As I'm leaving:
Tell your mama I need a raise.

+

My knife plumb
to a warped board, I set to core a tomato.

Imagine the slip
of teeth clean through,

the drip of seedy water
into the sink…

See the rabbi beam
as he tells me how,
after King's assassination,

The whole city sat shiva. No riots here.
My teeth tingle

with an anger he might not approve of.
He says *people are used to the lifestyle.*

It's so affordable.
Here, my money

gets me double
the bouquets of basil,

double the sinuous
summer squash.

I buy pounds of peaches
to slice at breakfast,

slurp alone
in the still afternoon.

Who did I choose
when I wished myself elsewhere?

Dear Memphis,

When my mother said my third brother was *alright, but*
the heat behind my cheekbones,
same as his cheekbones, bled out all sound.
I swiped to a photo of his kitchen window
where the cats I've never met
cackle at squirrels.

It takes a day
to reach my brothers now.
A week to scan fares, a sitter for my cat.

On the other cusp of this country, my first brother
signs on a house in the suburbs;
my second brother preheats
an oven the size of a doll's.
Last visit we plucked
his basil for pesto
and I learned I'm too old
to crash on the floor.
The ache in my sacrum
pulsed until it lulled—
bruised bones of our bones,
how gently you rock the soft organs we lifted off with.

Memphis,
you remember

how our grandfather
would wing us out of any waiting room
when he walked in and said we were his.

Enough with the Past, Let Me Deal with the Dead

Past the microphone, past the glass,
I clocked the resistant squint
cornering the old man's eyes,
the drawn-out vowels
same as my grandfather formed
to call the room to a halt.
Slow cadence: patience
to make them hear you.
He bought the table where I ate
my fill, where, to greet him, my syllables
clicked to half-speed.
                                        Yes, men
can be gentle.
                              Can be terrifying calm.

When the temple sold the plot downtown,
they left the bodies
and moved the stones. The hill taught me
how a rubbing holds
what a reading can't.
                                        The jaw wrecks itself:
taste the mineral edge
of a bone ground down in the clench.

Palinode after Family Movie Night

Tevye was a rich man.
His horse couldn't pull a cart,

but his own thick trunk
could steer the milk to town

and come home to a clean towel,
candlesticks at rest on the table.

No one fled.
A hundred years later,

my brothers and I settle
wheels of cheese into straw.

We mark the rinds
in Yiddish, a language

we breathe in, a language
we never abandoned.

Dear Memphis,

Do you get jealous?
Here, I walk
sweatless in the sunlight
and no one tries
to fry an egg on the sidewalk.

I had a good excuse
to visit, but the country
fell through.
The country where I am
is the country I abandoned:
same cracked concrete,
same magnolias.

At the edge
of my neighbor's garden,
I tipped
my face into her white flower,
her petals a palm
atop the layers
of cotton on my cheeks.
Each broad finger a shelter.

Descent Fragments

When we arrive, the rabbi says, *we make a cemetery first. Then a butcher, then a synagogue.*

When one gull sets off a sky-siren, I look toward a dozen chasing off an eagle. Is it that easy?

Is that why we burned our papers as our ships neared shore?

Aren't you descended from a famous rabbi? says E.

The rabbi says *Ashes to ashes*, but we don't cremate. Something about a body for the rapture.

No need to tell my husband about the motionless hatchling and bleaching its stain off our balcony.

Would you rather be exterminated or assimilated?

Between the eaves and gutters, clumps of death-come-quickly volunteer their blossoms.

Without a prayerbook, without ten for a minyan, I whisper the mourner's kaddish after the administration's first bombs.

I watch K worry her roving into matted shrouds before needle-felting the migrants: mothers, slim-limbed men, children.

We have a homeland now, the rabbi says.

Inside their fleeced radiance, flotation.

Palinode after Pharaoh's Decree

Instead of drowning,
the baby boys heaved in the Nile grew gills.

Their tongues
receded from suckle.

Their skin
wrinkled, shed.

Caves
of papyrus

swaddled
them.

Moses's reedy basket
shadowed their beds

and his body abided
their time

until the day
the river turned to blood.

The Boy on the Beach

My mother used to mutter
we'd *never be safe.* We must be
safer than they were.

I'm not supposed to say
how my father bought solid gold
Krugerrand coins

straight from the Denver Mint
and buried them in the backyard.
Southwest of the swing set: *Meet there if*

—no, *when*. My mother kept
our passports up to date; that part's
not a secret. *You can't just sit there.*

We learned the word *bystander*
to learn there are no bystanders. Not
my second brother

when I shoved my third. Not
in Germany. *We don't even know*
who we lost there. I do not want

to tell you about the four minutes
at sea: what the boy's weeping father
told the cameras. No distance

from the wreck itself, if you really look.
His body is on every screen.
You have to see the cavern

of his left eye socket glancing
the foam. You have to look for a flutter
in his lashes. The little shell

of his left ear opens upward,
but it doesn't hear the rolling surf
or the persistent scratch

of a Tunisian policeman's pencil
logging his body in a notebook
while his cheek presses into sand.

To Belong Less to the Aggressor

Shem means name, *Shmuel* the name
embossed glittergold
on the vault cover
lowered onto the coffin.

My tongue ululates
between palate and teeth
between eulogy and kaddish.

>

Grief sleepwalks,
lisping *yisgadal v'yiskadash*
toward Jerusalem. Toward Jerusalem
the scrolls turn like clockwork.

Through splayed roots
the river's fingers figure anthems:
we say sh'ma and v'ahavta
toward Jerusalem, aleinu
with a bow.
We linger.
The nightmare looms.

<

Portion follows portion
toward *a dispersion*
in all kingdoms.

Disperse, the order
before the recorder hits asphalt.

>

Dia, apart, *sperein*, to sow.

My mother's rabbi
says *Israel isn't* always *right.*

I let my father tell me
about the male prophets,
tell me God has
a masculine pronoun, tell me

manna in the desert is feminine.

<

Lamentations figures Jerusalem
as an abandoned woman
not beautiful, but visible.

In the Old City
outside the Arab Gate

I spoke *aquí, así,*

took another tongue

to belong less to the aggressor.

>

Dia, apart,

sperein, to scatter, like ashes.

The historian tells me *I am calling my senators*;

we are all shouting

STOP

into the wind.

Dear Memphis,

Used to be your greensky afternoons
told me I'd wake in the basement,
my mother having walked
my slept body
into the windowless dark.

All the doors closed
on six scents of mouth breath.
Damp wool. Gyre
of fan blades over our limbs.

There were sirens, but the sound
didn't rouse me.
We don't get storms like that here.

But Where are You From?

There are Jews in Memphis?
asks the boy
in the dormitory elevator.

Yes, I say,
and we wear shoes, too.

+

Before the quotas:
three percent,
then two;
before the literacy
tests. Before

the huddled masses
had to pass
Ellis
or Angel, maybe
get sent back,

a ship docked in New Orleans,
a portion of my people
in its hold.

Twenty years before
the Civil War,
we were never sold,
      were often turned away.

Before long,
we floated up
to Memphis
                    from where
             we came and went,
                          sometimes stayed.

+

             I thought diaspora was our word,
                          my father says
             over the front page.

             SHALOM Y'ALL
             painted on white tiles

             hangs just inside
             the mezuzah'd front door.

+

             In history class,
             a circle of junior evangelists
             surrounds my desk.

Bibles sit stacked, set
to thumb, thump. Here,
faith-based means *Christian.*

+

Off in New Braunfels,
Sarah, my grandmother's
grandmother,
grew up on a cotton farm,
then left for Chattanooga
when the weevil swarms snuck in.
Her daughter
Dorothy Rose married dairyman Harry Wise,
had my Grandma Harriet
in August of '33. Around then,
they moved to Lookout Mountain.

Each iteration ekes progress: abandoned
Civil War cannon in the front yard.
Dorothy's first miscarriage

around when my father's father's
Russian-born rancher
parents
cashed their cattle at a loss.

Poor Sarah and Benjamin.
Each step out
of pushcart-pogram country
unstable.

My Grandma Sylvia shadowed
possible shoplifters
down Illinois aisles of
                her parents'
Halpern Department Store,

her siblings and cousins dispersed,
                her zeyde
directing them in Yiddish.
Her sister Helen's still alive.

The last iron E cattle brand
is still in my uncle's metal shop
beside the plaster models of
                his father's hands.

+

The cashier cocks her head and asks,
Where y'all from? Before my father
comes out with our what,

I cut him off—*Here.*
We know when to pick up.

There are Jews in Memphis?
These days, fewer.

Dear Memphis,

Today my cursive
keeps skipping
its double-crests;
summer turns
to simmer, sun to sin.

I wanted to live
where no one knew
who I belonged to.
I wanted to tell you myself.

Where Else but Here

after the Migration Series by Jacob Lawrence

in the gallery

Expecting
a sequence
of ascent,

we pause
...Look at the suitcases...
shuffle-shuffle
...the white judge...

In the crowd's funnel
I scribble I
turn-shuffle-stop
at packed-in ticket lines
at whites with shotguns.

Travel is proceeding as it should
for those who should be traveling.

Over my pencil's scratch
I hear *Excuse me*
and retreat from the frame
to let a man past,

but he eyes my notebook, asks,

Do you know about this?

I say *some*

He asks,

Is it true?

I say, *Yes, it happened*

He asks, *How?*

panel 1

At the platform
every migrant's
                stiff overcoat

obscures a neighbor
-ing figure. Perhaps one

weighs the options:
St. Louis   Chicago   New York.

Perhaps another flees
a labor-hungry employer

                                        who remains
        outside the frame.

Features fade
into the movement,

each figure's capped brim
                                        shading
          another's profile.

Behind cross-hatched partitions,
sky's streaked

like washwater…
                To portray
the collective requires erasure.

panel 2

The white steam
shovel driver:
one hand on the lift, one on the throttle.

What do I know about exile?

I circle these panels
: these pasts
press on.

in the gallery

…You don't just say here you go *to children.*

…look at that engine…

…mmm mmm that skin
-ny little boy…

…are they thumbnails for something bigger?

…thumbs up or thumbs down?

Can I ask about your pendant?

…look at that nail…

…do you see the hammer?

panel 57

I sketch her roughly
                                        to scale.

Minus signs for knuckles:
those, I can handle.

My pencil struggles
to place the steep black rectangle

of drying rug or drape
                                        Lawrence brushed

from the top of the frame

                    to where her black arms depart
      from her shoulders, her

      perfectly bisected white shroud
swathing the washerwoman at work.

                              Am I allowed here?

I thicken the *57* on my version
of the frame's bottom right.

So close to the end
of the sixty. Still standing
with the cotton threads
                                                  she stirs…

I see her face split through—
her umber wash stick
sunk in the swell of opaque water
        into which she stares,

                        churning a turbulence.

Dear Memphis,

Last month
Minnie couldn't find coffee pods,
and I sent a year's worth. When her daughter
broke the blender, I sent another.
Well I thank you, she said.

Back when I would stomp
across the threshold,
Minnie set the iron on its end
and picked up her pink tumbler of tea.
Ice chuckled against the plastic
and I sat to relish
whatever easy scolding she'd held
for those minutes
before she drove off to her grandkids.

I picked at upholstery. Shot the shit.
Never folded
a single shirt, though I'd root
through the baskets to claim
my own—
bless my small body, that white child's ease
that I cannot, not ever, give up.
Well alright then, she'd smirk,
and collapse
the board.

Behind the fresh clothes,
                                        my mother kept
her stocks of just-in-case. Plenty
                         of salt and meat
we wouldn't eat
until the apocalypse.

                                  I've never written a check like
the one my mother sometimes forgot
so Minnie'd drop by on her day off,
                                                  one grandchild
                              on each hand,

each hand I've felt in the crease of my neck
but never held myself.

Dear Memphis,

        Today in the heat my eyes swam
as if through a chlorinated green.
My legs lagged,
                sticky like the seatbelt
my second brother jabbed
while we bickered
                    over whose sweat dripped on whom.

Even the pool water
            stuck like skin.
                        My brothers and I walked
thousands of strides from the locker room,
  our bare feet
                calloused chalk-white.

        One August day
the lifeguards lowered a block of ice
into the deep end,
            the great buoy risen
effortless above the sixteen-foot mark.

I watched
        other kids chase and touch

below the roped-off

springboard.

You couldn't bring guests.

The South I Know Best

In the kitchen, a cure of honey
curls over
what rot hasn't won yet.

Overnight, some creature
tumped over the feeder.
Seed pockmarks the walnut shade
where no grass grows.

On the other side of the hammock trees
low brick walls brushed white.
The dog bursts from the magnolia's tendrils

out a hole I can't slide through
no matter how deeply I bow.

The Portrait

New Braunfels, Texas

A gold chain   lassoes her neck
and drips   into her lap.

In oil paint, their eyes   look equal in age,

image splitting the difference
between her sixteen,   his forty-one.

On his upturned palm,

the lay   of her ringed right hand
seems to assure the viewer

she was willing.

>

In the parking lot I pass a rope
round and round, tying the frame to the roof rack
while my mother calls—

Tie a what *hitch?*
Won't it fly off on the highway?

I thread the end through a cinched-down loop
and lean into the tension.

>

Out the window, oil derricks prowl
a brown horizon.

A timber yard
marquee says *GOT LAND? LET'S BUILD.*

>

When the roof rack's *hoo roo*
ascends to a high *hee*

we pause at a pullout
                                        choked with cardboard and diapers
to re-wind the rope around the frame.

The signs say *RHINESTONE ANGEL,*
      SHE-WOLF DRIVE,   *WOMAN HOLLERING CREEK.*

>

We turn the painting over
to the small-town archive.

My mother insists
on a photo. I refuse

to smile. What she wants
taken care of
                    I want gone.

<

Where our ancestors
set their mill,

I watch an eddy circle
round and round,

mist of relentless motion
calling me into the stream.

I won't reach   for my mother's arm.
I won't paint another picture.

Dungeness

Beneath what I see is what I know.

When the dark sinks in,
drop a lantern off the dock.

What gathers looks, at first, like specks of dust,
then moths at a porch light in summer.

Stay put. Pass a bottle. The great beneath
keeps rising to the beacon,

brine breathing around us like a lung.
Disc of carapace. Fleck of claw.

A crab's shell starts out too soft
to be protection.

Think of the depth it sinks to,
fresh from the molt,

to bury itself in the sand.
I know how it feels

to realize I've bricked my own dungeon.

Dear Memphis,

Seasick in the car wash, I
gripped the wheel while
the lights changed: green
to blue to pink

and the neutral roll nudged
something rubber, something
untouchable inside…

there's comfort
in a constant ache.

My restlessness doesn't belong,
yet here it lives

where somehow the suds
smell like your dust,

your most volatile fragments inside me.

A liminary Art

an erasure

i.

The early history

wholly

sold under

cost.

fever

rough sense of demand for

pipes to flush

ii.

The committee considered
the River,

well sunk.

a flowing result, water

plying
the

interests
operative.

iii.

in

a tunnel in a

branch

in a

suction well

called " well." Worth

the

pressure

of purchase

as organ ,

its

drill

the stem

iv.

known logic
is

a shallow syncline,

stern

near its edge

Springs,
sand and gravel;

verses in succession

v.

page the Art Department

mum on
the pump

page
the
accord of State

the drill first
ate

plants
found
in

the
Auction . sons all dust

no records

remain

Clearing

A strung-up cable
bows for a lone cardinal
blown in early. Red

crown, leafless grey: indistinct,
all, to a color-blind boy.

A chickadee's twitch
lofts what limbs are left on a
pruned tulip poplar:

puffed-out wing-thing enmeshed in
the brittle logic of flight.

Aubade without Departure

Little more than a room, I
cling to myself. I press three fingers
inside one curved bone,
and they hold, as if fastened
to an edge of limestone
ages roofed from the rain.

When I lift my eyes
I can see past the first horizon:
I measure the mist as it sleeks out
of my belly, my belly hunched
like prey in the chase.

A bit of brightness.
I've folded slips of cloth
inside cloth, too slim to catch
the limbs already falling.

Five miles beyond the Wilderness Boundary sign

a chipmunk slinks
through the lakeside rootscape

: haunches to
hideout to

sneak up
& chew through
the thin plastic
that guards the peanuts
I lugged
from civilization
where foraging is leisure
—if I drop my vigil
to watch a bufflehead splash down;
if the flick that shoos a crow
scares off a chickadee;
if I unravel

the twist-tie
& offer the chipmunk a palm

-ful of fat & salt,
what else will I have ruined?

Slope Light

When I coasted
to the end of the runout
flat, the mountain
was its own cobalt
shadow. The white rose
around me, one
thumbnail at a time.
Remember how I skidded
like a flat stone. How long
did I bury myself
trying to stand?

After Waking

Close the window.   Lather   the scrim of ash
    from your hands. Watch   the satellites watch
the blaze   two hundred miles   from here, where
    a human hand   threw gunpowder   over a river.

        Live tissue   keeps glowing   into ember.

Wipe the counter.   Watch the dawn   shape
    haze into skyline: soot-black
and ash-bright,   city aspiring
    to a mirage   of whiteness.

        Scrape the cinders   of uprightness   from your eyes.

Swatch Test

Close one eye. Look
at the paint chip, then the wall;

paint chip, then wall. If you tick
back and forth quick enough,

the shade will cast an after-image,
your own eye speckling

the space you want to change.
I keep shaving my upper lip

even though it's hidden under
a mask, even though it will be

as far as I can imagine a future.
Close one eye. What would it take

to take in what you're repulsed by?
If I let the shadow grow back. Shade lingers

like the sulfur a matchstick leaves
when it's shaken out. Tick back and forth—

You can choose what you want to be ashamed of—
back and forth across the wish.

Sober Georgic

a cento

Suppose

the wine brings forth its buds; its leaves unfold

and the white stork, who's the scourge of snakes, is seen,
is flourishing for you, and the foaming wine…

Sour in taste. And, sour in aftertaste, suppose

the menacing shade grows thicker on the vines
enveloped in the darkness of its leaves.

Dig out a big pit in the solid ground.

Not merely for the pleasure of the prospect,
Earth brings forth from herself in ample justice

the wild uncultivated haunts of birds.

Dear Memphis,

Once, my grandma's mailbox toppled
                    in straight-line winds
                that tipped an old oak
  onto her roof—
burst the tomato pots
              she'd lugged up the ladder.

              From time to time, the metal caved
            at the hands
of someone's baseball bat.

    Her knobby wrist
used to dash a ballpoint
            across a legal pad—
slim pen loops
          to distances she'd mapped
on the butcher paper family tree.

             We used to turn old envelopes
    inside-out. We unstuck
                seams, smoothed
           creases. She pressed
 strips of tape
             against the folds I held
    with both hands, not a thought
                      to anyone's answer.

I'll never know
whose cursive burned
when we found
metal shards in her azalea,
a half-shell of duct tape
still intact from the homemade bomb.

Memphis, you know
what can tear through my words
when I send them
out into this weather.

Stone Way North

The crane's arm pivots, its cockpit
                    flag
          claiming the skyscape

above the old quarry. Now razed, the lot
                    holds
          a copse of scaffolds

for stories of steel. Across the street
                    I water
          rooftop beds: bleached

Sterilite tubs of kale and herbs,
                    rustproof
          aluminum trough

companion-planted with basil and tomatoes
                    (Brandywine,
          Sungold, and Gold Nugget

already in bloom). *What will you* do *with them all?*
                    my mother asks.
          Eat them, I say.

                              What will we do—love, you

selected the Pink Berkeley Tie-Dye
for slicing;
I, the Golden Rave for sauce.

What will we do with Sunny Goliath?
Black Cherokee
pulp to purple the mozzarella

on the nights when it's too hot to be
hungry.
When we sleep, only our toes touch.

When the chill returns, I'll stir
the sauce pot
while you seed and peel. Won't you,

over the simmer, soothe my shiver—
boil,
pour, and seal.

Christmas Eve

Round Rock, Texas

I *ma'am* my husband's aunts
like I think I ought to,

like my mother taught me
not to do my own.

She's always known
what to say to Gentiles

to set a moment at peace:
lengthen your vowels,

slow your speech.
Swallow the boozy laughter.

My husband unfurls
a tamale, and I kiss his cheek,

pink from mere minutes in the sun
while I sketched a stalk

of aloe stiff in death.
Don't let them hear me shiver.

The cat purrs, its left ear matted
with another beast's slobber.

No Matter, My Treads are Lined with Kevlar

My husband wants me
lit up like a rave kid,

so I click-click my muscles
into reflective skin.

Every day I blink-blink
to see, to be seen as a brightness.

Nobody knows me
when I spit into the curb.

Last summer
the mechanic called me over

and said, *You should know*
how to do this.

I leaned my ear to the hub.
He spun the wheel

and said, *You can hear it.* Turn the screw:
Now you can't.

Teach me this silence.
Click by click I clench tenderness,

barely a [_____]
to tell me when.

My knees pump; my rotors rumble
against the disc I need to clean,

and the wind chimes go [_____]
on East Aloha Street

and an engine revs
and a man is pumping his fists

into another man's [_____]
so hard I hear the [_____], [_____]

over the [_____] in my throat.
He can't know me

when I yell *What're you doing? What're you doing?*
—he just calls me [_____] and runs.

I Picture Meeting Myself, Age Eleven, Second Summer Away

At first I see the other girls skipping
ahead, a counselor stacking cones in the bed

of a golf cart and motoring off down the trail.
I haven't found you yet, though I know

you must be easing your tense stride
my way. Your first brother exists

on the other side of the cloudy
Mississippi pond no one is allowed

to swim in. Your elbows won't kiss his
until you're clicked in to your mother's Volvo

three weeks on. If you stood
together on the thin shore

each of the twenty-eight nights,
would you see the angel of death

sink out of reach? Something can't be touched.
Your mother's letters must steady her wavering voice.

At the edge of the field, I see you lift
your hand from the chain link fence.

You try to lower your foot so slowly
your knee won't know. How dearly you want

to unseal your lips. I want to drape
your arm across my shoulders, smooth

your Umbros and cotton shirt. Your limp
frays all over the path, and the gravel

makes it impossible to know which way
you might fall. When you lean

your torso on a dry pine trunk,
I crouch down and offer

my back to you. You climb on.
I clasp the outside of your thighs—

won't you let your chin rest: whisper the worst
of you into my neck, into the wreck of me.

What I Know of God

Benjamin sat in the dip between God's shoulders,
rocking side to side when God swung God's arms.
God's arms must be so tired. So strong. O God,
I cling to the back of your ankle where
your skin wrestles itself into folds. I've
made it hard to reach me. Benjamin held
your neck between his legs, his dick
at the base of your skull. Grown as we are,
we are still your children; we still stand tense
when your foot disappears in the sand. When
Benjamin entered the narrow place, how
did you turn from his hunger? The sight of
your face—it would kill us.

Dear Memphis,

You don't just start a fire;

you build it. I'd ring
her doorbell, eyes

having leaked
across my grandmother's root-pocked lawn,

and she would split

sheets from a stack of Sunday *Times*
to feed the red steel belly

she tended. Behind me,
my own home

bellowed in a blaze
I lit but didn't build.

Her wedding ring spun
behind a knuckle swollen like a knot.

Bark grows thick around a loss.
Slip by slip,

words toppled, inaudible in my throat.
She was still breathing

when my uncle asked who *might want the house*,

and I felt fire in the hollows
of my ears,

years' worth of sap
seizing my mouth shut.

The Tether

Miriam prayed

for the basket's weave

to hold, for the reeds

to hide her body

in the banks

of the broad and slow.

Around her brother,

a cloth their mother

had wrapped tight.

Two teetered,

every inhale a tug

at the end of a thread.

How do you say goodbye to a brother?

His body pushed

the water aside,

the sister into shadow.

How Prayer Works

No bread for us. Almost done dying,
my grandmother's bed hummed,
nurses' scrubbed arms winging
her fluids. She wouldn't stand for
all this serving, this kneading her limbs
like loaves while she shivered like

no bread. For us, almost done dying
was her eyes drug-hung, her feet swollen.
Her toes' motion nonsensical
like electrons in outer valences
that won't stop quivering. All her atoms
will reassimilate into body—

no, bread—for us almost done dying
of hunger. In Casablanca, roadside snail broth
slaked—*salaam*, *shukran*—on my throat swollen
with silence. I left her because I sometimes
do what I am told. I couldn't tell my brother
the news I knew was coming. No going home for us,

no bread for us. When she was almost done dying,
my mother told me I had to go cross
the ocean. I'd planned to. In flight, I tried

to write her a letter
and landed too late. I slipped a wedge
of bread in broth and watched it disappear.

Tangier: Before Crossing

I send my *salaam* into the bread stall. A woman in white points to the clock: quarter-to-eight. I finger my last dirams; she turns back to her board where, out of a loose mound, she kneads a fugue: fold, quarter-turn; fold, quarter-turn; fold, quarter-turn; fold, quarter-turn—how long have her hands known the dough-skin's yield?

Three iron griddles steam.

Out of a gust of children, a boy jumps aside. The sleeve of his uniform brushes my elbow as his chin juts across the counter. He bellows a greeting. The woman responds in tones that my ears take as scolding, then hands him a wedge of foil-wrapped cheese. He runs on. I scribble him

onto my linen-bound page.

I watch her lift a linen off a row of risen domes. Her fingertips crawl under one puff, easing it off the board, and when it spills as if to tear itself in two, her palms become its platforms; her wrists draw circles through the powdered air, white sleeves orbiting her forearms. *Slap*, the slack body on the scalding disc. The dough inhales beads that bubble, that will yield in my teeth as

I ferry off her continent.

Dear Memphis,

I used to pace the terminal
at my connection:
high windows in Detroit; Atlanta tunnels
to put off
the sight of my grandmother's friends
at the gate, the weight
of their jewelry
laid upon my hands.

After services,
my grandmother's palm
would graze my spine
as her friends drew in,

friends with coral lips
while hers smiled bare.
She pressed
her arm to my arm,
head to my head
to dull
my need to be right
and have them know it.

Think of all the thank-you notes
for lace I gave away.

Think of all the women who mailed me
clips of my name
in the paper,
who walked with her,
her bunions
eating through her shoes.

Try and keep track
of the women
my grandmother drove
to the doctor, women
who swam her same slow mile
at five AM.

After Granddad died
she missed daylight savings
and got to the pool at four.
Sat in the parking lot: *Why go home*
when I'd turn right back around?

At the shiva, the women
made me a plate for the plane.

Passage

Long canoe of the womb,
eddy out;

the river is dropping.
Cavelike,
                    the turtles

have tucked away
for the evening.

The moon beams
back at herself

from the belly of a current
you were barely scraping by on.

Womb, wait where you won't mind
the gravelly shudder.

Don't ask
if our erosion

is a die-off.
Don't ask if we've arrived

at our dead end.

Stakeout Station

Rows of translucent
ova line his lab
bench: Heliconius,

the butterflies
my first brother has flown
halfway down the globe

to coddle. He
worries the hatch,
microscope trained

on one
exterior.
Lens to nest.

No way to guess
if a specimen is sick
or cross-bred sterile

yet. As long as
something comes out,
it'll come to use.

In the images he sends,
I fixate on his fingertips.
They're slim like mine

and steady as he drops
liquid beads
from his pipette

to the eggs' rest.
While my hands tremble
at the finest tasks,

his hold. He has always
felt a pull toward
fatherhood. I'm too cold

to be called maternal.
While this set gestates,
its forebears

need him
to trellis
passion vines

under mist nets,
to seed their water
with pollen and sweet.

For him, they swaddle
themselves in silk
and emerge, winged

for slaughter. For him,
the scalpeled
abdomens. The tweezed

ovaries.
The spread
-sheet he's left with

to conjure
their species'
odds of survival.

Nocturne

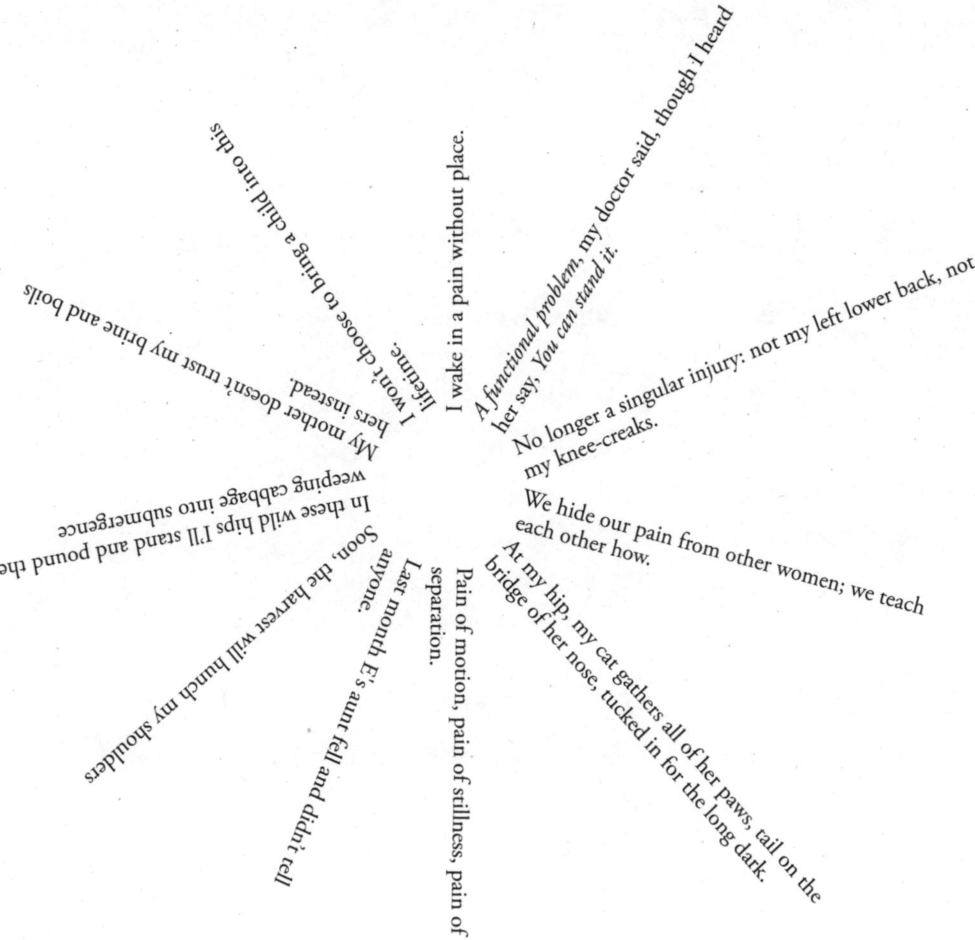

I wake in a pain without place.

A functional problem, my doctor said, though I heard her say, *You can stand it.*

No longer a singular injury: not my left lower back, not my knee-creaks.

We hide our pain from other women; we teach each other how.

At my hip, my cat gathers all of her paws, tail on the bridge of her nose, tucked in for the long dark.

Pain of motion, pain of stillness, pain of separation.

Last month E's aunt fell and didn't tell anyone.

Soon, the harvest will hunch my shoulders

In these wild hips I'll stand and pound the weeping cabbage into submergence

My mother doesn't trust my brine and boils hers instead.

I won't choose to bring a child into this lifetime.

Dear Memphis,

I still like my hair pulled.
Since I lost the length,
I scratch along my scalp
to get a grip.
I used to cling
to my breakfast chair
while rubber teeth ripped
through my curls.

Broken strands floated
down to linoleum;
hands trained not to let go.

Still, I stiffen
my neck. A net knots
around a wish
to be smoothed into place.

So many mornings
Minnie must've swept
my hair off the floor.

Once, while my mother squeezed my shoulders,
Minnie held
the smoldering end of a match

to my scalp,
but the tick had already fled.

So many hours
buffing our fingerprints
out of the polished wood.

I'd sometimes sit
for her to braid my hair,
her touch so light
I couldn't tell she'd finished.

Down This River

When did I learn downpour was this river's provenance?
Not to worry over water; Memphis won't tap out

unless limestone faults below the superficial loess.
My grandma's stubby thumbs buttoned my brothers and me

in rubber. I slid open her glass back door to trudge the ditch
chasing down from her magnolia. Blizzard, her springer spaniel,

spun and jumped. Our steps galoshed, dislodging cobbles
fast as the ditchflow ridged them free. Mud-lush, the Mississippi.

We hopped the blowdowns. She carried the thickest boughs
downstream to where we'd dam the six-inch tributary. She couldn't top

a hundred pounds soaking wet, but there she was, skyflow
dripping in through her cracked slicker. The drainage

spilled through the chain link fence and over the drowned front yard
toward the curbside gutter of Waring Road,

named for the first sewage director to pump this swamp
and filter it for those who made it through yellow fever.

We bulked our bough-dam up with mud.
Behind it, a pool began to plump,

ran over. Each breach dropped silt that built
the levee anew. In the trough of it we stood

tall enough to resist the current, but still too small
to comprehend how frost pricks through millimeters of buffer.

How her toes creaked and tingled. How, when she and I
slipped in hip-high, out I'd carry her.

Notes

"Palinode after Family Movie Night" is in conversation with Joseph Stein's musical *Fiddler on the Roof*, based on Sholem Aleichem's "Tevye the Dairyman" stories.

"The Boy on the Beach" is in memory of Alan Kurdi, z"l.

"To Belong Less to the Aggressor" owes a debt to Maeera Schrieber's book *Singing in a Strange Land*, particularly her study of Lamentations in "'Where are we moored?' Adrienne Rich, Irena Klepfisz, Lament, and its Diasporic Aftermath."

"Where Else But Here" is in conversation with the *Migration Series* by Jacob Lawrence, a series of sixty paintings depicting Black Americans' escape from racial terror in the twentieth-century Jim Crow South. The line "Travel is proceeding as it should for those who should be traveling" was spoken by a Trump administration official on January 27, 2017, after the signing of Executive Order "PROTECTING THE NATION FROM FOREIGN TERRORIST ENTRY INTO THE UNITED STATES" which resulted in cancelled visas, extended detentions, deportations, and mass protests.

"A liminary Art" is an erasure of "A Preliminary Report on the Artesian Water Supply of Memphis Tennessee," US Department of the Interior, Geological Survey Water-Supply Paper 638-A, 1931

"Swatch Test" contains a line from Corinne Manning's story "We Had No Rules," from their eponymous collection.

"Sober Georgic" is a cento, a poem made out of the lines from other poems. Its lines come from Virgil's Second Georgic, translated by David Ferry.

"I Picture Myself, Age Eleven, Second Summer Away" is after "I Dream of Meeting Myself, Age Seven, County Fair Field Trip" by Geffrey Davis

"What I Know of God" is in conversation with Deuteronomy 33:12, "Of Benjamin he said: Beloved of the Eternal, he rests securely beside the Holy One. Ever does the Divine protect him, as he rests between the shoulders of the Infinite." That line expanded and moved me in a spiritual practice facilitated by mads deshazo z"l.

"Passage" is after "Night Repairs" by Molly Spencer.

"Down this River" is for Harriet Wise Stern z"l.

Acknowledgments

Thanks to the editors of the following journals for publishing poems from this book in various forms and sometimes under different titles:

About Place: “The Boy on the Beach” and “Five miles beyond the *Wilderness Boundary* sign”

Beloit Poetry Journal: “To Belong Less to the Aggressor” (finalist for the Adrienne Rich Award) and “Descent Fragments”

Day One by Little A: “Palinode after Pharaoh’s Decree”

Foundry: “Stakeout Station”

Great River Review: “Nocturne” (runner-up for the Pink Prize)

Lockjaw: “A   liminary   Art ”

Mantis: “Clearing” and “Stone Way North”

Muzzle: “Dear Memphis (You don’t just…)”

Narrative: “Return,” “Dear Memphis (When my mother said…),” and “Enough with the Past, Let Me Deal with the Dead”

Nimrod: “No Matter, My Treads are Lined with Kevlar.” (semi-finalist for the Pablo Neruda Prize)

The Pinch: “How Prayer Works”

Poetry Northwest: “Dungeness” and “Swatch Test”

Poetry Online: “Christmas Eve”

The Seventh Wave: “Dear Memphis (Do you get jealous?),” “Dear Memphis (Today in the heat…),” and “Dear Memphis (I still like…)”

The Threepenny Review: “Down This River”

West Branch: “The Portrait”

Wildness: “Passage”

"Dungeness" was reprinted in the anthology *Cascadia: A Field Guide Through Art, Ecology, and Poetry* (Mountaineers Books, 2023).

"Swatch Test" was republished in *Guesthouse*'s series "Relish: An Internet Archive"

Blessed is the source of life who has kept us alive, sustained us, and brought us to this season.

I send a river of ongoing gratitude to the people who shaped this book and my life in poetry, some of whom I name here, all of whom I carry with me:

To Susan, Jim, Nate, Jonathan, and Andrew Edelman; to Minnie Hamilton: thank you for helping me write into our lives and histories. Ciaglos, Edelmans, Speros, and Sterns, your love holds me together.

To Jonathan Huey, mi corazón, steady harbor, loving cue to the present.

To my writing partners, Gabrielle Bates, Keetje Kuipers, Abi Pollokoff, and Preeti Vangani, whose consistent insight shines all over my words.

To the teachers who tended to me and helped me tend to myself: Linda Bierds, Daniel Hall, Tekla Harms, Marisa Parham, Steven Becton, Michele Phillips, Rachel Shankman, Lori McFalls z"l, and Lisa Sikes.

To my grandparents z"l: Samuel Edelman, Sylvia Halpern Edelman, Dr. Thomas N. Stern, and the singular Harriet Wise Stern, my model for lyric as a way to love.

To Temple Israel Memphis, a Jewish home for my family for five generations; to R'Micah Greenstein and R'Harry Danziger for sitting for interviews; to archivist Jen Kollath for hosting me and holding my grandmother's papers.

To the University of Washington MFA program, Mineral School Artist Residency, Crosstown Arts Artist Residency, Tin House Summer Workshop, and the Whiteley Center.

To generous readers at pivotal times: Catherine Bresner, Gabrielle Calvocoressi, emet ezell, Shelby Handler, Anna Hogeland, Patrycja Humienik, Jessica Jacobs, Ainsley Kelly, Shelby Kinney-Lang, Shara McCallum, Erin L. McCoy, Patrick Milian, Aimee Nezhukumatathil, Claire Schwartz, Alex Streim, and Lena Khalaf Tuffaha.

To Emily K. Cole: dear, deep channel of friendship.

To Amorak Huey and Han VanderHart of River River Books: Your transparency, accountability, and care create oceans of possibility.

To my colleagues, my book club, my neighbors; to Kadima Reconstructionist Community; to organizers for free movement of all people across all (imposed, impossible) borders. To everyone working toward Palestinian liberation and return.

To my students: thank you for teaching me to listen.

To you: wherever you find yourself, wherever you're longing for.

Rachel Edelman is a Jewish poet raised in Memphis, Tennessee who writes into diasporic living. Her poems have appeared in *Narrative*, *The Seventh Wave*, *The Threepenny Review*, *West Branch*, and many other journals. They have received material support from the City of Seattle's Office of Arts & Culture, the Academy of American Poets, Mineral School, Crosstown Arts, and Tin House and finalist commendations from the Adrienne Rich Award, the Pink Poetry Prize, and the National Poetry Series. Edelman earned a BA in English and geology from Amherst College and an MFA in poetry from the University of Washington. She teaches Language Arts in the Seattle Public Schools, where embodiment and care root her personal, poetic, and pedagogical practice. Read more at rachelsedelman.com.